OUTDOOR SCIENCE

FORCES

Sonya Newland

WAYLAND

www.waylandbooks.co.uk

First published in Great Britain in 2019 by Wayland

Copyright © Hodder and Stoughton Limited, 2019

Produced for Wayland by
White-Thomson Publishing Ltd
www.wtpub.co.uk

Editor: Sonya Newland
Design: Rocket Design (East Anglia) Ltd
Illustrations: TechType
Consultant: James Thomson

ISBN: 978 1 5263 0946 4 (hbk)
ISBN: 978 1 5263 0947 1 (pbk)
10 9 8 7 6 5 4 3 2 1

Wayland
An imprint of
Hachette Children's Group
Part of Hodder & Stoughton
Carmelite House
50 Victoria Embankment
London EC4Y 0DZ

An Hachette UK Company
www.hachette.co.uk
www.hachettechildrens.co.uk

Printed in China

Picture acknowledgements:
Big Blu Books: Mia France 8–9 (all); NASA: 4bm, 15b; Shutterstock: Jose Luis Stephens cover tl, Izf cover tr, muhammad afzan bin awing cover bl, Sergey Ginak cover br, elina 4tl, supergenijalac 4tm, REDPIXEL.PL 4tr, Infinitum Produx 4bl, Pat_Hastings 4br, Sergei Primakov 5tl, Brian A Jackson 5tr, ShutterStockStudio 5b, wickerwood 6t, Rashevskyi Viacheslav 6b, udaix 7tl, Digital Storm 7tr, Veronica Louro 7b, Zaitsava Olga 10t, Aleksandar Grozdanovski 10bl, Svetlana Foote 10br, Alones 11t, Krithnarong Raknagn 11bl, GLYPHStock 11bm, Various-Everythings 11br, Pajoy sirikhanth 12t, Lars Lindblat 14tl, Aris Suwanmalee 14tr, Ninya Pavlova 14b, Gtranquillity 15t, Steve Cordory 16t, Sashkin 17b, OBprod 18t, Marc Bruxelle 18b, Chireau 19tl, AlexZaitsev 19tm, Wuttichok Panichiwarapun 19tr, dies-irae 19ml, All For You 19mc, ElectoneXSeries 19mr, Hong Vo 9b, Alena Stalmashonak 20t, Perfect Gui 22tl, Sergey Ginek 22r, wavebreakmedia 23t, jointstar 23ml, Christian Musat 23mr, TukkataMoji 23bl, Quang Ho 23br, NokHoOkNoi 24t, magnax 26t, Mr. SUTTIPON YAKHAM 26m(1), Malll Themd 26m(2), Crepesoles 26m(3), Dragol Kostadinov 26m(4), udovichenko 26b(1), Marilyn Barbone 26b(2), picsfive 26b(3), Alex Staroseltsev 26b(4), Craig Walton 27t, Snowbelle 27m, Scandphoto 27b, alextan8 28t.

Illustrations on pages 12, 13, 16,17, 20, 21, 24, 25, 28 and 29 by TechType.

All design elements from Shutterstock.

Every effort has been made to clear copyright. Should there be any inadvertent omission, please apply to the publisher for rectification.

The website addresses (URLs) included in this book were valid at the time of going to press. However, it is possible that contents or addresses may have changed since the publication of this book. No responsibility for any such changes can be accepted by either the author or the publisher.

Contents

What are forces?

A force is a push or a pull on an object.

Forces everywhere

Forces are at work all around you. You can't see them, but you can see what they do. Forces are what make things speed up, slow down or stay where they are. They also make things change direction or change shape.

Types of force There are lots of different forces.

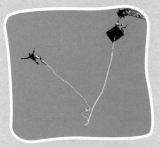

Gravity pulls objects towards each other, or towards the centre of the Earth.

Friction slows objects down as they rub against each other.

Air resistance is friction between air and an object moving through it.

Water resistance is friction between water and an object moving through it.

Thrust pushes a plane or rocket forward as it takes off.

Magnetism pulls some metals towards each other.

Weak or strong?

Forces can be weak or strong. If you push something, it will move. The harder you push, the faster and further it moves.

Heavy objects need a strong force to move them.

Light objects can be moved with a small force.

Special forces

Most forces only affect an object if they touch it. Gravity and magnetism are special. They can affect objects without touching them.

SPOT IT!

Look around you. How many different forces can you see working?

Measuring forces

We describe forces by their size and their direction.

Newton's newtons

The size of a force is measured in newtons (N). This unit is named after a famous British scientist called Isaac Newton. One day he saw an apple fall from a tree. He started wondering why it fell downwards instead of sideways or upwards. Newton realised that the Earth's gravity pulls everything towards it.

Which way?

When you push something, it moves away from you. When you pull something, it moves towards you. When you throw something in the air, it moves upwards – and then downwards. Forces always work in a certain direction.

Arrows show the direction of a force.

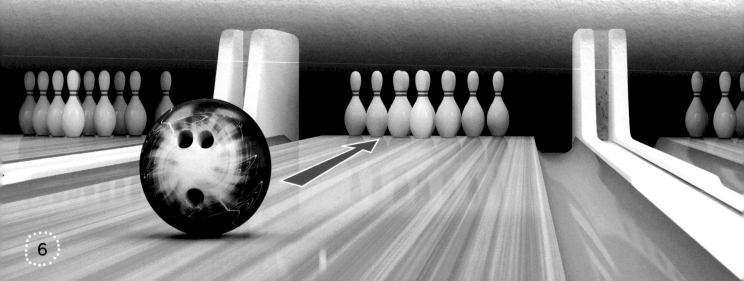

Balanced and unbalanced forces

Forces work in pairs. If two forces are the same size, they will not change the way an object is moving. If one force is bigger than another, the object will start moving or get faster.

balanced forces

The force of gravity pulling the book down is equal to the force of the table pushing up.

unbalanced forces

The force of the engine is bigger than the force of the air resistance, so the car speeds up.

Working out forces

If you know how strong each force is, you can work out the total force and direction. Think about a tug of war.

If one side is pulling to the left with a force of 4 N ...

... and the other is pulling to the right with a force of 3 N ...

... then the total force is 1 N to the left.

Playground forces

A playground is the perfect place to watch forces at work!

You will need:
* a swing
* a friend

Step 1

Stand behind an empty swing. If you don't touch it, the swing will hang straight down and not move.

Step 2

Apply force to the swing by giving it a gentle push. Is it easy to push?

Step 3

Watch the swing:

✳ Does it move quickly or slowly?

✳ Does it go a long way before coming back, or just a little way?

✳ What eventually happens if you don't touch the swing again?

Step 4

Now give the swing a stronger push. Does it go higher and faster than before? This time, when the swing comes back give it another strong push. Does it go faster? Notice whether it goes even higher than before.

WHY NOT TRY? Have a go on the roundabout. Do you feel a force 'pushing' you outwards to the edge of the roundabout as you spin?

Step 5

Let the swing stop, then ask your friend to sit in it. Repeat steps 2 and 3. Do you have to push harder (apply a stronger force) to get the swing moving? As you keep pushing, watch how fast and how high the swing goes with your friend in it compared to when it was empty. Why do think that is?

SPOT IT!

What other forces can you see at work in the playground?

Making things move

Without forces, nothing would move!

Keep moving

What can you see moving around you? The wheels turning on a bus? A dog running down the street? Clouds drifting across the sky? Things move because they are being pushed or pulled along by forces.

Bicycle wheels move when force is applied to the pedals.

Getting faster

Forces can make something go from standing still to moving very quickly. This increase in speed is called acceleration. Some things move faster than others.

HANDS On!

Have a running race with a friend. Can you feel yourself accelerating? Eventually you stop speeding up. You are running as fast as you can. After that, you move at a constant speed – or you get tired and slow down!

You can move faster than a snail ...

... but you wouldn't beat a cheetah in a race!

What a drag!

Thrust is a force that sends a rocket or plane up into or through the air. Thrust works in the same direction as the vehicle is moving.

Drag is a force that acts in the opposite direction to thrust. It is caused by air resistance (see page 22). Drag makes a machine slow down.

For the rocket to launch, the thrust must be bigger than the drag.

drag

thrust

Making forces bigger

Simple machines are used to make small forces bigger. They can make objects move further and faster.

Here are some simple machines.

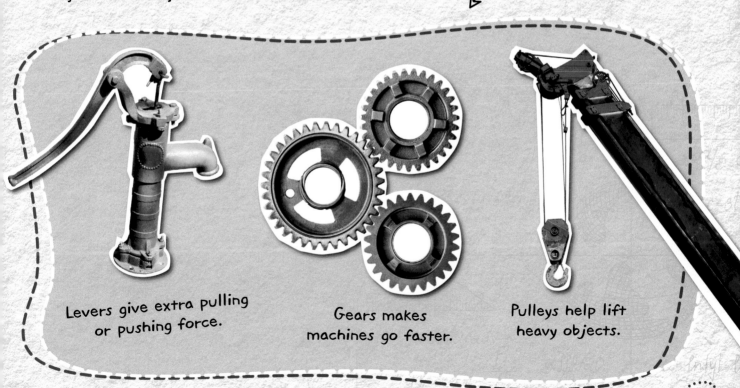

Levers give extra pulling or pushing force.

Gears makes machines go faster.

Pulleys help lift heavy objects.

Make a bottle rocket

See thrust in action by launching your own rocket!

You will need:
* ✳ a piece of thin card
* ✳ an empty plastic bottle
* ✳ cardboard
* ✳ scissors
* ✳ sticky tape
* ✳ water
* ✳ a cork
* ✳ a pump with a needle connector

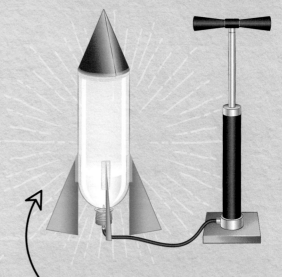

Step 1

Roll the card into a cone shape that will fit on the bottom of the bottle. This is the 'nose' of the rocket. Cut the cardboard into three triangles. Use the sticky tape to attach them to the neck end of the bottle to make the fins.

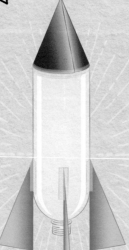

Step 2

Fill the bottle about a quarter full of water. Push the cork tightly into the top of the bottle to seal in the water. Carefully push the needle of the pump through the cork. Make sure it goes all the way through.

Step 3

Put your rocket on an outdoor table or on the ground, ready for launch. Slowly begin pumping. Watch what's going on inside the rocket. You should see air bubbling into the water.

Step 4

Keep pumping until your rocket blasts off! What happens just before it does? What happens when all the water has gone?

! REMEMBER

* Get an adult to help you cut the fins out of the cardboard.

* Don't stand right over the rocket in case it goes off by accident.

* Make sure your rocket is pointed away from people and buildings before setting it off.

FORCES AT WORK

* The bubbles were building air pressure inside the bottle. When the pressure got too great, the cork popped out.

* The water and air shooting out of the end created thrust, and the rocket launched.

* Once all the water was gone, the rocket slowed down because drag was greater than thrust.

* Eventually it was pulled back to Earth by gravity.

Attractive gravity

Gravity is a force that pulls things together.

Sticking together?

Everything has gravity – your house, the ant on the garden path, even you!
But all these objects are small, so their gravity is very weak. That's why
you're not stuck to the person sitting next to you. Your gravity isn't strong
enough to pull you together.

Huge objects like planets exert a
lot of gravity. The Earth's gravity
pulls all the smaller objects near it
towards its centre. That's why things
fall downwards when you drop them.

The Earth's gravity pulling on you is
what keeps your feet on the ground.

Orbiting planets

In fact, gravity is what keeps the whole solar system
moving. The Earth's gravity pulls on the Moon and
keeps it moving around our planet. The Sun's gravity
pulls on the planets and the planets pull back. This
keeps them in orbit around the Sun.

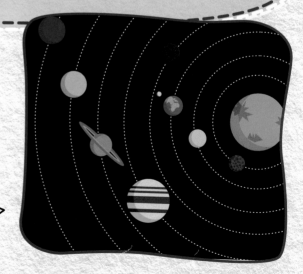

Mass?

How much gravity something has depends on how big it is. What we mean by that is how much mass it has. The mass of an object is how much 'matter', or stuff, it is made up of. Mass is measured in grams or kilograms.

When you weigh something, you are actually measuring its mass.

SPOT IT!

Can you spot the tide going in and out? This is caused by the Sun's and the Moon's gravity pulling on the sea.

Or weight?

Weight is not the same as mass. Weight is a force – the force of gravity on an object. It is measured in newtons.

An object's mass stays the same wherever it is, but weight changes depending on gravity. There's no gravity in space, so astronauts are weightless, but they still have mass.

Spin the bucket

Defy gravity with this simple experiment!

You will need:

* a bucket with a handle
* water

Step 1

Fill the bucket about two-thirds full of water. You are going to spin this in a circle so it goes up in the air. Before you start, what do you think will happen to the water when the bucket reaches the top of the circle and is upside down?

Step 2

Pick the bucket up by the handle and start swinging it by your side. Begin making small arcs from the ground towards the sky. Gradually make the arcs bigger.

Step 3

Keep going until you are making full circles with the bucket. Keep spinning the bucket in the same direction at a steady speed. Make sure your circles are smooth.

Step 4

What happens to the water in the bucket when it's upside down? Was your guess correct? Why do you think this is?

FORCES AT WORK

* When the bucket is still by your side, gravity pulls the water down towards the Earth.

* When you spin the bucket in a circle, you create a force that pushes the water outwards, away from the centre of spinning. This happens even when the bucket is upside down.

* What do you think would happen if you stopped the curved motion of the bucket?

⚠ REMEMBER

* Make sure you're standing well clear of other people so you don't hit them with your bucket.

WHY NOT TRY? Repeat the experiment, but put a tennis ball in the bucket instead of water. Does the ball fall out?

Surface friction

When two objects rub against each other, they create friction.

Slow down!

Friction makes objects stick together a little bit. That slows them down. If there's enough friction, an object will eventually stop moving.

Rough and smooth

The amount of friction depends on the surface of the objects. Rough surfaces create more friction than smooth surfaces.

Wheels reduce friction. This skateboard will roll more smoothly and for a longer time before friction slows it down.

SPOT IT!

Watch someone ice skating. Why do they move smoothly and quickly?

Different surfaces

Look at these surfaces. Which one do you think creates the least friction? Which one creates the most?

gravel

snow

sand

ice

wood

carpet

Get a grip!

It is more difficult for things to move when there is a lot of friction. But rough surfaces are easier to grip on to. The friction between the ground and your feet is what stops you falling over.

Trainers have thick rubber soles with patterns on them. These grip the ground well so you don't slip when you're running.

HANDS on!

All objects have energy. An object in motion has energy of movement. If friction slows it down, that changes to heat energy. Try it yourself. If you rub your hands together, they get warm. That's friction. You feel some of it as heat.

Testing surfaces

Find out more about the friction created by different surfaces.

You will need:
* ✳ two bricks
* ✳ a piece of cardboard
* ✳ a toy car
* ✳ a stopwatch
* ✳ a tape measure
* ✳ a notebook and pencil

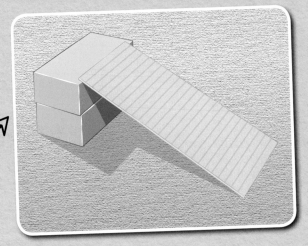

Step 1

Find a large patch of grass outside. Put the bricks on top of each other and put the cardboard up against them to create a ramp.

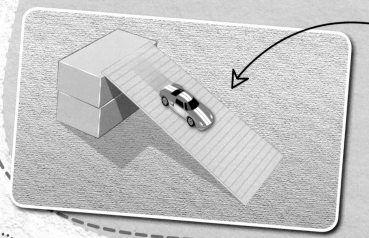

Step 2

Put your car at the top of the ramp and let it go. Ask a friend to start the stopwatch as you release the car. They should stop the watch when the car has come to a complete stop on the grass. Make a note of the time it took from start to finish, in seconds.

Step 3

Use the tape measure to measure how far the car travelled in centimetres. Measure from the bottom of the ramp to where the car stopped.

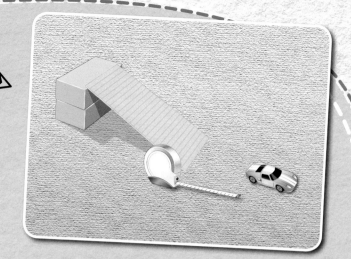

Step 4

Repeat the experiment on different surfaces. Try:

* gravel
* paving stones
* sand
* soil
* tarmac
* any other surfaces you can find

For each surface, write down the time and distance the car travelled.

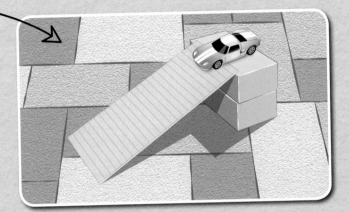

Step 5

Draw a table to compare your results. Have columns for:

* the type of surface
* the time in seconds
* the distance in centimetres

FORCES AT WORK

* When you let go of the car, gravity pulls it down the ramp, towards the Earth. It accelerates as it goes down the ramp.

* When it reaches the grass, friction between the grass (or other surface) and the wheels begins to slow it down.

Repeat the experiment with the ramp at different angles. Add bricks so the ramp is steeper each time. Are the results the same? If not, what differences are there? Why do you think that is?

Air and water resistance

Air and water resistance are both types of friction.

Moving through air

Air resistance acts on objects that are in the air. They might be ...

flying ...

... or falling.

Drifting down

Air resistance slows things down. There's hardly any air resistance on something falling freely, so it falls really fast! A parachute creates a big area for air to push against. This slows the fall.

Moving through water

Water resistance works in a similar way. The force of water slows down an object that is moving through it. Water resistance acts on everything from boats to fish.

When you swim, you can feel the water pushing against you.

Streamlined shapes

Large, flat shapes create a lot of resistance. Machines built to travel quickly usually have a streamlined shape. That means they are thin and pointed. Streamlined shapes travel more smoothly through air and water.

The *streamlined shape* of fighter jets means they can travel faster than the speed of sound.

Penguins have narrow, straight bodies so they glide through water easily.

Make paper planes in different shapes. Which one travels furthest and most smoothly? What is the most streamlined shape you can come up with?

Create an egg parachute

Test the effects of air resistance with this egg experiment!

You will need:

* a black bin bag
* scissors
* string
* a hole punch
* three eggs
* three sandwich bags

Step 1

Take the black bin bag and cut three squares out of it. They should be:

15 x 15 cm

30 x 30 cm

60 x 60 cm

These are your parachutes!

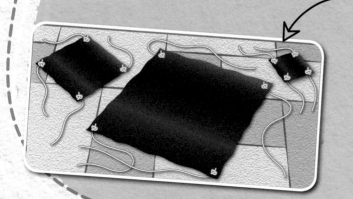

Step 2

For each parachute, you need four pieces of string the same length as the sides. So, cut four pieces of string at 15 cm each, four at 30 cm and four at 60 cm. Punch a hole in all four corners of each parachute. Put a piece of string through each hole and tie a knot at the top to secure it.

Step 3

Put an egg in each sandwich bag. Twist the top of the bag shut. Tie the end of the strings on each parachute around the top of a sandwich bag with an egg inside. Look at your prepared parachutes. Which one do you think will carry the egg safely to the ground?

Step 4

You need to drop your parachutes from quite high up. Try a second-storey window or the top of a climbing frame. Drop your parachutes one at a time. Make sure that you drop each one from the same height.

Notice what happens to the parachute each time. Does it fill with air? How long does each one take to reach the ground? How many of the eggs broke? Did you guess correctly which one would carry the egg safely?

FORCES AT WORK

* When you release the parachutes, gravity pulls them down towards the Earth.

* Air resistance pushes up, slowing them down. Because larger surfaces create more resistance, the biggest parachute will drop more slowly than the other two.

! REMEMBER

* Make sure the ground below you is clear before you drop your egg parachute!

* Be safe when dropping your parachutes. Never lean out of a window, and make sure you are holding on properly to a climbing frame.

Amazing magnetism

Magnetism is an incredible invisible force.

What is a magnet?

A magnet is anything that attracts magnetic objects. Magnets come in all different shapes and sizes. You might have seen these magnets at school.

u-shaped magnet

bar magnet

Magnetic materials

Most materials are not magnetic. Only certain types of metal are magnetic.

magnetic

not magnetic

HANDS on!

Find out which everyday objects are magnetic. Find things made of different metals and hold them close to a horseshoe magnet. Can you feel the magnet 'pull'?

North and south poles

All magnets have two 'poles' – a north pole and a south pole.
The magnetic force comes from the poles.

Opposite poles attract
(pull towards) each other.

The same poles repel
(push away from) each other.

Earth – a giant magnet

The very centre of the Earth is a huge ball of metal. As the Earth spins, the metal ball sends out a magnetic force that travels around the planet.

The Earth's magnetic force

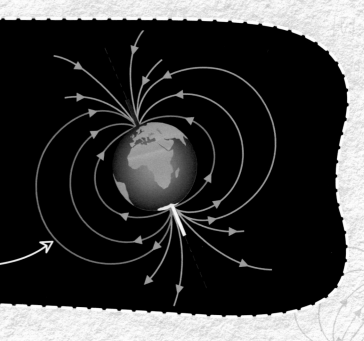

Finding your way

Have you ever used a compass to find your way? A compass contains a tiny magnet. The Earth's magnetic field pulls on the magnet so that it always points north.

The Earth's magnetism helps animals that travel long distances find their way.

SPOT IT!

Magnets are used in all sorts of machines. How many things can you see that use magnets?

Make a compass

Follow the Earth's magnetic field by making your own compass.

You will need:

✳ two needles

✳ a bar magnet

✳ a piece of paper

✳ thread

✳ a pencil

✳ a glass jar

Step 1

Take one of the needles and rub it along the south pole of the magnet 40–50 times. Don't rub it back and forth – slide it in the same direction each time. Repeat with the second needle.

Step 2

Tape the needles in a piece of paper and fold it over to seal it. Mark one end S and the other end N.

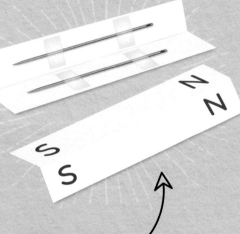

Step 3

Tie the thread to the middle of the pencil and attach the other end to the paper with the needles in. Balance the pencil across the top of the jar, so the paper hangs freely inside it.

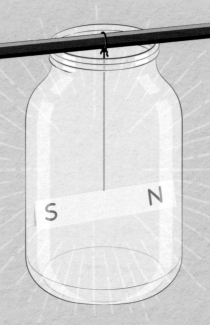

Step 4

Stand still and watch as the 'magnet' spins to show you where north is. Which direction is your school or house? Go for a walk. Move about in different directions. See how the needles move so that they are always pointing north.

! REMEMBER

＊ Be very careful when holding the needles. Make sure you don't prick yourself.

Glossary

acceleration – how quickly an object is speeding up

air pressure – the 'weight' of air on an object

air resistance – a type of friction that acts on an object travelling through air

attract – to pull together

compass – a device that contains a magnet, which helps people travel in the right direction

drag – the force caused by air resistance that slows objects down

friction – a force between two objects that are moving against each other

gravity – a force that pulls two objects towards each other

magnetic – describes something that attracts certain metals

magnetic field – the area where the effects of magnetism can be seen or felt

magnetism – a force that acts on magnetic materials such as metals

mass – how much matter, or 'stuff', an object contains

orbit – the path that objects in space take around other objects, such as the planets moving round the Sun

repel – to push apart

streamlined – a thin, pointed shape that reduces air or water resistance

thrust – the force that pushes a plane or rocket forward

tides – the rise and fall of the sea throughout the day

water resistance – a type of friction that acts on an object travelling through water

Further reading

Books

Forces (Boom! Science)
by Georgia Amson-Bradshaw (Wayland, 2018)

What are Forces? (Discovering Science)
by Kay Barnham (Wayland, 2018)

Forces (Science in a Flash)
by Georgia Amson-Bradshaw (Franklin Watts, 2017)

Websites

Follow the links on this page to find out about all different types of forces.
www.bbc.com/bitesize/topics/znmmn39

Check out this interactive site for loads of facts about forces and motion.
www.dkfindout.com/uk/science/forces-and-motion/